From the Gutter to God's Pulpit

Healed and delivered from hurt,
heartbreak, and betrayal
and then transformed and
catapulted into favor, grace, mercy,
and a faith-filled and totally
dependent life with the Almighty God

Sandra Adona-Durham

ISBN 978-1-0980-6211-8 (paperback)
ISBN 978-1-0980-6212-5 (digital)

Christian Faith Publishing, Inc.
832 Park Avenue
Meadville, PA 16335
www.christianfaithpublishing.com

Printed in the United States of America

W rite your book, for you have many people to help, heal, deliver, and encourage. For I told you that the hurt, broken, broken-hearted, and tormented souls will come before you, as I (God) have given you the power to heal and deliver as only that kind of *power* and *anointing* that you have been given only comes from me (God) as not many people on earth have the kind of *power* and *authority* that I have given you. For to whom much is given, much is required. For the pain, trials, and tribulations that you have endured are great; for the reward and blessings that I will bestow and place upon you are far greater than anything you can think or imagine. Hold onto me, for your change is coming and sooner than you think. For I (God) love you and you are the apple of my eye, for I know what I am doing.

For the mouth of the Lord has spoken to you on this day October 10, 2017. Weeping may endure for a night, but *joy* cometh in the morning.

Quotes: Quotes noted in the book are quotes that got me through those times or when I read or heard the quotes, took me back to the place and time that I went through, when I was going through some of the toughest times, trials, and tribulations of my life, which have been many. But God, had a plan for my life and the tactics and schemes that the enemy and man tried to use to destroy me, God used it to fill me with his wisdom, power, anointing, and strength. Those quotes also took me back to that time and place and assisted in the choosing, calling, trials, and tribulations, intervention, healing, deliverance, and catapulting process and the writing of this book

Songs: Songs noted in the book are songs that got me through those times, or when I heard the song, it took me back to that time and place and assisted in the choosing, calling, trials, and tribulations, intervention, healing, deliverance, and catapulting process and the writing and producing of this book.

Always remember, God loves you the most and no human can love you like God can and does.. Open yourself up and allow his love, power, anointing, and wisdom to flow in and through you. We all have a calling for the upbuilding of God's kingdom!

1

The Calling

"The Call" by Isabel Davis
"To Worship You I Live" by Israel Houghton
"Hope in Front of Me" by Danny Gokey
"Walk on the Water" by Britt Nicole

A strong woman is the lifeline of her family. She carries within her the power to endure pain and courage to sacrifice. She has the power to create and nurture life. She is indeed the epitome of love and sacrifice.

—Aarti Khurana

Never forget: How far you have come. Everything you have gotten through. All the times you have pushed on even when you felt you couldn't. All the mornings you got out of bed no matter how hard it was. All the times you wanted to give up but you got through another day. Never forget how much strength you have learned, gained and developed from and through God. God's strength is made perfect in your weakness.

—Power of Positivity

A strong woman is one who is able to smile this morning like she wasn't crying last night.

—Harriet Morgan

I opened my eyes at 6:00 a.m. on October 10, 2017, now a widow at fifty years old. I had always been a wife, mother, confidant, caregiver, teacher, chauffeur, amongst many other things to and for my family for the last twenty-five years. I am now waking to an alarm clock going off, kids to wake up for school, and a job and career to tend to. As I woke with a heavy heart (still thanking God for waking me and being in my right mind) wondering and asking God, "God I have totally surrendered my life and being to you, being a good mother, a good friend, a faithful worker in the church, a dedicated worker in the medical field and my children in every way possible to ensure that they reach their goals, dreams, aspirations, and become high achievers in school and in life. Why have I been betrayed by family, people who I thought were my friends, kids acting like they are losing their mind, and with a husband who has now been deceased for seven months?

After being married for twenty-five years and always having that soul mate to talk to and exchange thoughts, ideas, and decision-making with, I am now faced with waking every day and making major decisions concerning my children, career, and my household totally on my own (in the earthly realm of things, but in the spirit realm, always having God to talk to and walk me through the days, nights, and decision-making process).

After being in a marriage with a man who was truly a man, a true gentleman as well as things that were the norm for me, and now realizing that I often took for granted (waking every morning to tell me just how much he loved me, always told me how nice I looked and how good I smelled before I left for work in the morning, ran my bath water, massaged my feet, went to all the boys' football games, quit his job during the day to obtain a night job to ensure that one of us were always home with the kids, washed clothes, did the dishes, making sure that I always had something cold to drink in the summer and hot to drink in the winter before I could get through the door from a hard and stressful days work most of the time). One who always supported me in whatever I did, even if he didn't agree with it or thought it wasn't the right time to do so, and a man who *always* protected myself and his children and would go to any lengths to do so, no matter who or what it was or what it entailed.

I found myself being and feeling completely betrayed, hurt, and heartbroken and having to hold on to the walls and closet doors after getting out of the bed, which was extremely difficult just to make it to the bathroom to get ready for the day. Hurt more so by the friendship that was compromised, betrayed, and trust that was completely destroyed, and not by the relationship or intimacy that we shared (first boy I ever loved, lived with, and fell in love with) but by someone who I truly thought was my friend and only to find that the gambling habit, women, selfishness, and many of the demons that lied within him, took precedence and priority over any friend-ship and/or relationship that we ever shared on hand, past or present. Someone who I thought had my back at one of the most difficult times in my life and had ever faced.

Only to find that he knew I was vulnerable, lonely, now a single mom to four kids and an individual who took all the information and vulnerability that they were aware of, ran with it, totally used it to their advantage, and completely went ghost, without a trace, no goodbye, no more phone calls, no response to my text messages, no answer to my phone calls, and no answer or response to my voice-mail messages at a time when I needed someone to talk to, vent to, obtain advice from the most, and after a two-hour conversation the night before and thinking that everything was fine (at least I thought I needed all these things from a person).

At that very moment is when God started speaking clearly to me and I knew that it was *truly* time to let it go, surrender my life, being and everything that I had and everything that was in me to God as I realized that my life was spiraling out of control with what I was doing and being with the person that I was with. I realized and God revealed to me that the relationship that I was in, *the devil tried to kill and destroy me* and God told me it was being done so subtly, that I didn't even know what was going on. God told me I was going to hell and he had to snatch me out, which was painful and hurtful. It didn't feel good at the time, but I knew it was for my good, and I knew that God did it. I had stopped going to church as I knew that my pastor would be able to look at me and pick up in the spirit as to what I was doing and who I was involved with as God had blessed him with a strong spirit of discernment and the prophetic gift.

The one person that I trusted, welcomed into my home, introduced to my children and husband, sat at my table and ate my food, told my most interpersonal feelings, trials, and tribulations, hurts, concerns, tears, prayed with and for and cried to during the wee hours of the morning, when I couldn't sleep (after my husband's passing) was the one who did the unthinkable. When I needed her the most, she also went ghost for weeks, told untruths right before me and in my face, and only later to find out that she befriended the one who betrayed me, and that she was the one who performed the ultimate betrayal.

She realized after not hearing from me for weeks, calling, and texting and trying to reach me, but to no avail, is when she realized that I knew what she had done and who she had done it with. Till this day, I pray for both of them (which wasn't easy in the beginning), wish them well as I asked God to bless them and give them the desires of their heart. The blessing for me is God allowed me to truly forgive, love, and not hold any anger, bitterness, or hatred in my heart for either of them.

Since the ultimate betrayal, I have been far beyond blessed, elevated in God, promoted on my job, great bonuses, and my relationship with God has grown, deepened, and has become so intimate, it amazes even me at times. What man meant for evil, God will turn to good! (Genesis 50:20: "You intended to harm me but God intended it all for good." He brought me to this position so I could save the lives of many people) and as love covers a multitude of sins.

I then knew that I would and was going through a process as God told me that he was going to catapult me into the next level in him and that I needed to trust him, hold on to his unchanging hand, and to follow him as he said he had called me for such a time as this. I had not been just called, but chosen, and there was no turning back, and that I had no more time (many are called, few are chosen).

I knew and God told me he had set me apart from the very beginning of my being (even when I was in my mother's womb). Growing up, I always felt different, like I never fit in or belonged (no matter where I was, who I was with or what I was doing) as God told me that's why I never felt a part of anything or anybody, because he had set me apart for a reason and because of the great calling on my life.

Once I completely surrendered and truly said yes (a true, heart-wrenching, for real, *yes*) is when God revealed himself to me more than ever before (as I have always had a relationship with God where he started speaking to me and giving me dreams at the age of twelve years old) and told me what my *true* calling and choosing was, and what I had been chosen to do for him and his kingdom. I can remember locking myself in my room at fourteen years old and not coming out until I memorized the Lord's Prayer.

The very day on Sunday, September 24, 2017, was when I truly said *yes* and my life has never been the same. All of me, my being and my life, completely belonged to God. God completely isolated me from family, friends, and relationships, and it was just *me* and God. It was a lonely process but a very necessary one. I was being tried through the fire (kids, family, friends, and work) and I knew (even though it didn't feel like it at the time) I would come out shining as *pure gold!*

God spoke clearly to me on that day, God told me that the platform had been set, my kids were safe in his arms, there were no more excuses (God had been calling me for years, but I ignored the calling) and there was no turning back. At that point and time, my life belonged completely to God, and it was no longer my own.

My circle of friends is very small (I have never had many friends and I was always okay with that simply because I don't take the word friend or friendship lightly) which is why I am and have always been very careful of how I choose and use the word *friend*. God has placed three individuals in my life who I am truly blessed to have and I thank God for them on a daily basis as I know they pray for me and hold my arms up when I am feeling weak and weary. My circle is very small (the circle of friends that God implemented, planted, and made for me), *but powerful* and through prayer, fasting, trusting, believing, and having the utmost faith in God, God gave me the people that I asked him for, and exactly the people that I needed. The circle I made for myself were chickens and God replaced them and placed eagles in my life. Chickens can't stand and are jealous of where you are, what you are doing, where you are going, and what you have accomplished. Chickens look and stare at what you have and have accomplished and can't even give you a compliment or tell you that you are doing well or that they are proud of what you have done or are doing.

Eagles pray and fast for you, cry with you, hold you up when you are weak, and tell you the truth even if it hurts your feelings or your heart. Eagles think, love, talk, and dream on a completely different and higher level and are not jealous or envious. When an eagle connects with other eagles, *power comes forward*. While chickens peck on the ground for anything they can find, eagles soar and fly in the air way above ground and hold up other eagles.

On November 15, 2017, I went to Connecticut on travel for a week to a little town by the name of New London. Not knowing at the time this was certainly a set-up by God. The hotel was a small hotel in the middle of nowhere that sat all by itself. The hotel had just been renovated as the phone in the hotel room was not working due to the renovations that had just been done. The cell phone reception in the room was horrible, and you either had to stand by the window and burn up from the heat coming from the heater, or freeze if you turned the heat off to hear the person on the other end of your cell phone (as it was terribly cold in Connecticut, twenty degrees and below every day), so I chose not to talk on the phone, only to contact my children daily while I was away. God set me up to spend all that time with him (just me and God) and the encounters with God were different on a daily basis. I went from asking God why had I been betrayed by family and people who I thought were my friends, to by the end of my trip, praising and worshipping God and thanking him for taking the people out of my life to thanking and praising him for the people that he replaced them with. The last evening that I was on travel, God spoke and communed with me, and I communed and spoke with him from 10:30 p.m. until 4:00 a.m. in the morning, and by the time I opened my eyes and awakened for departure from my trip, I saw things, life, nature, work, hurts, betrayals, and people in a completely different way. As I had always been used to being in a relationship and married for twenty-five years, from that day forward, I knew that I didn't need a man or to be in a relationship to make me whole, and that I was perfectly fine with it just being God, myself, my children, my two dogs, and my home.

My pastor and my first lady, whom I love dearly and have come to know personally, welcomed myself and my family back to my home church with open arms and with no questions asked after leaving and being away from my home church for over two years. When my husband passed away, they did not hesitate when asked to preach my husband's eulogy (that's a man of God, a first lady, and a church after God's own heart). A few of my church members rallied around my family and me as if we never left and with no questions asked; they did whatever needed to be done.

A job of which I had been with the organization for a total of twelve years, and then left for a total of six months, and when God told me to go back and to call my chief nursing officer to return to the organization as before departed from the organization for another job opportunity. My chief nursing officer, who is not easily impressed or one who will not welcome you back with open arms (whom I love dearly) told me that I always had a job with the organization, asked me not to leave the organization, and stated that I could always come back (which again God allowed; with this organization, it is not easy to return, and for the most part, you are not able to return under any circumstances). As I returned to the organization, I was welcomed back with open arms, a great raise, and even was allowed to keep my tenure as if I had never left for a total of twelve years (Now tell me that's wasn't God, because I know without a shadow of a doubt that it was).

Upon my return home from a week of travel and my encounters with my Almighty Father, my life was and has never been the same. I was given a new director for my department on my job; she was certainly God sent and one who I truly love (as she stated that she had no choice in the matter and was ordered by God to come to and join the organization). She has been and is a true blessing in my life as she has poured into me professionally and certainly spiritually.

I inherited a true and honest friend (God will remove a chicken and replace the chicken with an eagle), who doesn't and will not tell me what I want to hear, but what I need to know and all that he does, says, and portrays, has to line up with the word of God. I have known this true man of God for several years as a professional, and he has now become a true friend and confidant who I can talk to about anything without judgment, nor am I ever worried or concerned about hearing anything that we discuss repeated to anyone other than ourselves. He has certainly shown me how a real man treats a lady without any expectations, without wanting or expecting anything in return, just an honest and true friendship which entails being true to yourself, honesty, and accountability. This is a man who is a true gentleman who I have always admired for his business and entrepreneural mind, honesty, integrity, character, faith in God, his commitment to his family, and his genuine love and care for his mother (look at how a man treats his mother and that's how he will treat his female friend(s), his woman or wife). Upon losing my husband and he losing his mom (the person in our lives who were closest to us) placed our friendship and trust for each other on a greater level. Other than God, this is one person who I listen to and take advice from when given, as I know he seeks God in all his decision-making, whether it is a business or a personal matter. He prays for me as I pray for him on a daily basis. We seek advice from each other, consider each other's feelings in what we do, and the decisions that we make, and we can be ourselves (good, bad, or indifferent) and we laugh and joke constantly as he is my true friend. I have never had a true male friend who I wasn't in a relationship with as now I know what it means to have a true male friend with no expectations, hidden motives, or agendas. This is someone I can call early in the morning or late at night and just say, I need to talk or I have a dilemma and I need some advice and before we talk, his response is always, "Let's pray about it and see what the Lord says and let's ask God for the wisdom to make good decisions." If I'm exhausted from a hard day's work and state that I'm a little tired, this is a person who instantly starts praying and tells me after prayer that we, not I, but we are going to be all right.

2

The Choosing

"Gracefully Broken" by Tasha Cobbs
"If Not for Your Grace" by Israel Houghton
"Already Been to the Water" by Vicki Winans
"God Is Here" by Martha Manuzzi

Let them judge you. Let them misunderstand you. Let them gossip about you. Their opinions aren't your problem. You stay kind, committed to love and free in your authenticity. No matter what they do or say, don't doubt your worth or the beauty of your truth. Just keep shining like you always do. (Scott Stabile)

There's going to be very painful moments in your life that will change your entire world in a matter of minutes. These moments will change You. Let them make you stronger, smarter, and kinder. Don't you go and become someone that you're not. Cry; scream if you have to. Then you straighten out that crown like the queen that you are and keep it moving.

—Erin Van Vuren

She slept amongst wolves without fear, for the wolves knew a lion was amongst them.

—R. M. Drake

A woman is like a diamond. She reaches her full potential under immense amounts of pressure.

—Entity

As I sat in church on Sunday, October 1, 2017. During praise and worship, the Lord started speaking, and I started writing and these are the words he spoke to me:

"For I have chosen you for such a time as this, the broken, broken-hearted, hurt, and tormented souls will I send before you. I (God) know what I am doing for I chose you even before you were in your mother's womb. I (God) chose you from the very beginning, that is why you never felt a part of anything, no matter where you were, what you were doing, or who you were with. For I (God) have given you the power to cast out demons as I confirmed to you many years ago (God gave me the power to cast out demons when I had to take the power and authority that God had given me to cast a demon out of one of my children). For I (God) will place my chosen ones in position as those who have placed themselves in positions that they should not be in, for the demise has come and I (God) will expose them. For I the Lord have set the platform for you and anyone who tries to divide or demise the platform that I have set, will be turned over to me (God). Those who have hurt and betrayed you will come to you for help as you will be the only one that can help them, for I (God) will ordain it that way and you will do the *work* and be of assistance to them. Unblock all numbers from your phone and keep your lines of communication open.

For the discussions have already started about you (the lies and the attempt of defamation of your character) and I the Lord will take care of them and the discussions that are being held. For I the Lord say to you, be silent and say nothing even when you know they are talking, for I the Lord will hold them accountable.

I (God) am setting the platform for you, it's time to stand and proclaim in the name of the Lord. I, the Lord say to you, for you will preach and teach the gospel as I will prepare you. For the broken, broken-hearted, and hurt people will come before you, and I (the Lord) will give you the power to heal and deliver and you will have the power that I (the Lord) will and have imparted in you to heal the land, for the prophetic word has been spoken, given, and imparted in you by me (the Almighty God). Get ready, for your time has come and sooner than you think, to stand before my people and proclaim the gospel of Jesus Christ (the almighty, all-knowing, all-healing, all-delivering, all-concerning, all-providing, all way-making God). For again, get ready, get ready, for I (God) will promote you, not man, so don't look to man for the promotion, look to me (God), for I (God) have set the platform for you to take your place in me (God). For the mouth of the Lord has spoken.

I always had a really good, loving, close, and genuine relationship with my dad growing up. At the age of thirteen, my dad remarried and everything started to change. I saw what was going on and no one else in my family saw it (the prophetic gift that God gave and imparted in me). I didn't understand this gift and didn't realize it was a gift due to the fact the I didn't have anyone around me who was spiritually inclined to inform me what the gift was all about. I always felt different growing up and felt that no one understood me (that's how the enemy works, tries to make a child of God feel inadequate).

I always had resentment and jealousy from the women who were attracted to my dad because they realized and knew the relationship we had—I adored him and he adored me. When the enemy found a toe whole, which became a foot hole, and the foot hole became a stronghold, and that's when the enemy came in and was allowed to destroy the relationship between my dad and myself as I would see and notice the smirks, laughs, whispers, and conversations as they thought they had won. I made the decision to leave my dad's house and moved in with my older sister (the enemy thought he had me).

At the age of nineteen years old, my sister introduced me to my first drug dealer male friend, who soon became my drug dealer boyfriend and a man who was forty years my senior. This fast, adulterated life, became my life quickly, which entailed drugs, lots of money, fast cars, designer handbags, clothes and shoes, diamonds and gold, lots of gifts, and lots of favors from many people (as he was big in the drug scene). This life came with a very high price and cost that I didn't know about, didn't think about, nor cared about at the time (everything cost and there is a price to pay).

After being in this relationship for one and a half years, I found out about his wife. I was the other woman for one and a half years with no knowledge that I was the other woman. I was always at his apartment, which is where I practically lived (I did have a place of my own), and his wife had the house and the kids. One summer day, as I was heading out for a shopping spree with a girlfriend of mine, the phone rang, and I answered it. The woman on the other line said hello and I said hello. She said, "May I speak to William?"

I said, "Who is this?"

She said, "Tell him his wife called," and hung up the phone.

I called him and informed him of what conversation had just occurred and his statement to me was, "You almost made me lose everything I have."

At that point, I made the decision that he had just lost me (I loved him, but I loved myself more than I loved him). I was young and realized that there was better for me. I had a good job, made good money and I wasn't going to settle nor lower myself or my standards and have a boy (A real man wouldn't have done myself or his wife that way) treat me that way.

I told my girlfriend what happened and we gathered everything that was mine, left, and left his keys on the table. He called and called and called. I never answered his calls and he continued to ride through my neighborhood. After all that failed (as he had keys to my place), I was at work one afternoon, and when I came home from work, he had brought some things that I didn't realize I left at his place. By that time, I didn't care what I had left, laid them in the middle of my bed, and later that night called. I answered the phone, thinking that it was someone else (there was no caller ID then, only answering machines), and heard his voice. He asked me, "Did you get the things I left on your bed?"

17

I said yes and told him, "You forgot something, you forgot to leave my keys." I hung up the phone. He continued to call my home, call my job, and drive through my neighborhood, trying to convince me that he was in love with me; he would leave his wife and kids and wanted to marry me and make it work. At that point, I didn't care anymore, no longer loved him, and was actually disgusted and turned off by his immaturity and childish behavior and told him to move on with his life without me because I had moved on.

I called the telephone company the next morning, got my number changed, the locks changed on the door, and moved on with my life.

For the next five years, it was drug dealer after drug dealer, shopping spree after shopping spree, club after club, and weekend after weekend in New York. I had been seeing someone as we were great friends, and actually we became best friends where we helped each other with our issues, difficulties, joys, and victories in life as we celebrated and supported each other. We spent hours on the phone, hanging out, talking about what we wanted out of life, and wanted the best life had to offer. He was always at my house or I was at his house. Our friendship was a great friendship as we had never been together intimately and could and would talk to and be there for each other through anything and everything, and he wasn't bad on the eyes either as plenty of women wanted him. We always had the utmost respect for each other, and when around or out with each other, neither of us ever flirted or talked to anyone else of the opposite sex, and with the dynamic and great friendship that we had, it was like no one else was ever around or with us but us two, no matter where we were or what we were doing.

One night, three years later, he needed to talk and I was there for him as I had always been; he came to pick me up and we laughed, talked, ate, and looked at each other for quite a while and we both confessed about how we felt about each other over the years. One thing led to another as we ended up with each other intimately as I heard angels singing as we were together and when all was said and done, he looked into my eyes as we laid in each other's arms and said, "That was the most beautiful thing that I have ever experienced."

We saw each other on occasions, we were still great friends, and with no strings attached.

Several months went by and I became sicker and sicker, especially in the morning and realized that I was pregnant. I called him and told him I needed to talk to him, and as always, he came right away and at that time I was already doing heavy drugs and had been for several months. I told him that I was pregnant and he informed me that he had just gotten back together with his son's mother (I was very well aware of the babies mama as well as the baby mama drama as he and I always talked about the issues with his situation and we would come up with solutions to the issues and problems).

He in turn asked me what I wanted him to do and I told him that I didn't want him to do anything. We talked for a couple of hours and when he left, he never heard from me again, except nine months later, when I called him from the hospital and told him that I had just had a baby and that he was the father. He was shocked and unaware as I guess he thought that I had an abortion. I had no intention of doing so and was certainly capable of taking care of my baby. He came to the hospital with his brother and was really upset with me as he informed me that he wanted to be there for his son.

At that point, the medical staff at the hospital informed him that our son had plenty of drugs in his system, which infuriated him even more as I had never seen him so angry and upset in all the years that we had known each other. Our son had to be swaddled from the drugs for a week and had to stay in the hospital incubator for almost two weeks (God still had his hand on me as my baby came home healthy, all limbs and not mental or physical dysfunctions as I had no prenatal care during the entire pregnancy and saw no physician).

I had still done hard drugs throughout my pregnancy as I hid my pregnancy from everyone including my family and my job as I did not show a great deal through my entire pregnancy and could still wear my regular clothes.

My sister, as we were living together at the time, tried to talk me into giving my baby up for adoption (the same sister that introduced me to my first drug dealer boyfriend). I was so messed up in the head from the drugs that I was actually thinking about and seriously considering adoption. One of the nurses at the hospital came and sat down and talked to me as she held my face in her hands and said to me, "Don't you ever let anyone talk you into anything like that." As she and her husband had to adopt a child as she couldn't have kids of her own. I thought about it and thought about it and said, "I can't give my baby up," (again the enemy thought he had me and used my sister to try and trick me).

At that point my mom and one of my other sisters heard about the adoption, my sister came to the hospital and told me, "Me and Mom are going to take the baby and if you decide to give the baby up, we will keep him and we never want to see you again."

I informed her that I couldn't give my baby up for adoption and as I was released from the hospital, I went and talked to my mom, I was scared to because she never knew I was pregnant. My mom embraced me with opened arms and said, "Bring the baby here and you, your sister, and *I will work together and raise my grandson.*"

Once my son was released from the hospital, I went to my mother's house and my sister and mom showed me the ropes of caring for a baby. I realized I loved being a mother and motherhood was the best thing that ever happened to me. Once my son came home from the hospital, the drugs, partying, and the drug dealers stopped immediately as my son was the most important thing in my life and I loved being a mother.

I was on maternity leave and had been at home (which was my mom's house) for two weeks caring for my son, when I heard a knock at the door. I went to the door, asked who it was, and the voice of a female answered, stating that she was a nurse from the hospital coming to see how I and my newborn son was doing. I opened the door and welcomed her in; she stayed for about thirty minutes. She came four times in a three-week period (randomly). Upon the fourth visit from the person claiming to be a nurse, as this time, she stayed a bit longer (almost an hour). We talked about motherhood, how I was feeling, and how I felt about being a mom and a single mom. After our long conversation, she stated to me that everything seemed to be going really well for myself and my son, and that she felt that her job and report had been completed, and that she was pleased with the way I was taking care of my son. I really seemed to love motherhood and that she could see the deep, genuine love and care that I had for him.

Afterward she sat and wrote a report and said that everything was complete, and then she rose from the chair, turned to me, gave me a big hug, and said, "I am so proud of you," and then left. I then realized that she was a social worker from the state, coming to see if I was still indulging in drugs as well as investigating if I was capable of taking care of my son or whether my son should be taken away from me to be awarded to the state.

Once I realized what had been taking place—I was so caught up in being a good mother to my son in whom I love so much—I fell to my knees and looked at my son's adorable face as he slept so peacefully on the living room couch. I cried out to God, thanking him for allowing me the chance to be a mother to my son (as I realized at that time that he was not mine, he belonged to God, and God entrusted him to me to be a mother and trusted me to take care of him) which is a huge honor in my eyes, for God to choose me to be his mother and for me to be God's daughter. He trusted me for such a great task and that God delivered me from the one-and-a-half-year drug addiction, snatched me from the snare of the enemy (even then, God was working when I didn't even know he was) and that he, the Almighty God loved me just that much.

3

Trials and Tribulation

"Speak to My Heart" by Donnie McClurkin
"I Go to the Rock" by Whitney Houston
"Alabaster Box" by Cece Winans

I am a strong woman. Everything that's hit me in life I've dealt with on my own. I've cried myself to sleep. Picked myself back up and wiped my own tears. I have grown from things meant to break me. I get stronger by the day and I have God to thank for that and God was in the midst of it all (lessonslearnedinlife.com).

Be strong and wait on the Lord. Be brave and trust in his plan. Because even when your plan falls through, his plan for your future still stands (Trust the Process Quotes).

She stood in the storm and when the wind did not blow her way, she adjusted her sails.

—Elizabeth Edwards

You are never too broken for God to use your story (deliberate women).

You survived what you thought would kill you.
Know straighten out your crown and move forward like the queen you are (She Conquers).

The Lord said to me: "For again, I have chosen you for such a time as this, eyes have not seen and ears have not heard. Get ready, get ready for leave all worries, concerns, trials and tribulations to me, for my yolks are easy and my burdens are light. I am catapulting you into the next level in me (GOD). For the enemy will try to trap and trick you again. For when you feel this in your spirit and see it with your spiritual eyes, not with you spiritual eyes that have now been opened, call on my (God) mighty name and I will and have planned a route of escape for you."

Life seemed to be looking up for me. I was the mother of a beautiful baby boy, I found a good babysitter for my son upon my return to work, and I finally gained strength and accepted the fact that I would be a single mother. Upon my return to work after being on maternity leave for six weeks, I walked into my director's office; we gave each other a huge hug, and she told me that she was happy that I was back. She asked me to take a seat in her office, she sat there for a few minutes and my heart was pounding as I didn't know what she was preparing to say to me. As I sat there, she looked me in my eyes and told me that my sister had come to pick up my check a month prior (as I had requested her to do so). She continued to inform me of how my sister had come to her office, collected my check, and proceeded to talk about me like a dog as well as told my director all my personal business. I had and have always been a very private person, professionally and personally. My director's exact words to me were and exactly quoted, "There is no way that I could or would ever have gone to my sister's job and boss and talked about my sister, the way your sister talked about you, your sister talked about you like a dog."

I was hurt, devastated, and felt totally betrayed once again as I shouldn't have been surprised as this was the same sister who turned me on to drug dealers, cocaine, and tried to talk me into giving my baby up for adoption (the devil thought he had me, but God had a plan for my life).

I proceeded to work for the government and walk through the halls and offices with my head held up high as I saw the smirks, snares, and heard the gossip. I went home, told my mother and my sister what my sister had done, and by the time we all finished talking about what happened, my anger and hurt turned to laughter as I felt saddened for my sister. Clearly there was something wrong with her, and there were certainly issues as I wondered how someone could be so mean, vindictive, hurtful, and evil toward someone that shared the same DNA.

A few months later, as I was asleep in the bed, I woke up to my Mom and my sister arguing, screaming, and yelling at each other. I got out of bed and proceeded down the hallway to see what was going on as harsh words and emotions were raging between the two of them. I asked them to calm down and asked what was going on, my mom turned and looked at me, told me to mind my business, cursed me out, and told me that I could take my baby and myself and get out of her house. I sat in the bedroom in disbelief and no understanding as to what had just happened and wondering where I was going to go and what was I going to do. A couple of days later, I called my dad and asked if I could come home for a while until I got myself together and situated so that I could get my own place for myself and my son. My dad told me that I could always come home. A few days later, I moved my son, myself, and my belongings to my father's house.

Almost a year and a half went by, my son was turning two years old and things were going great. My dad and I re-bonded and talked about all that had taken place with us in the past and my son had a great relationship with his grandfather.

One Sunday afternoon as my son and I had just come home from church and I was in the process of cleaning and cooking and preparing us for the week, my dad told me he had a female friend who he had been dating and that he wanted me to meet. Later that evening, as he brought her to the house, I looked at her and said hello, my spirit instantly picked up on who and what she was, what her motive was, and what she was all about (here we go again, but God had a plan for my life). We proceeded to sit at the kitchen table and ate dinner. I just listened to her talk and speak and kept my thoughts and what I knew to myself.

Several weeks went by. My father walked in the house one Saturday afternoon and said, "We have company." He moved her and her fifteen-year-old son in the house that very day. Upon her moving in, the jealousy and the plotting between her and her son began. Several weeks later, I had a conversation with my oldest sister and proceeded to tell her about the situation and what was going on as I was saving money and preparing to move into my own place. My sister told me to move in with her as she knew exactly who she was and what she was all about. Upon my return to my dad's house later that night—it was cold and raining—I entered the house and proceeded to get ready for bed as I had to go to work in the morning.

My dad knocked on the door to my bedroom, entered, and told me that he needed to talk to me. I walked into the kitchen and sat down at the table. My dad stood there and stared at me for a few moments. He told me that he had ruined one marriage for his children and he wasn't about to ruin another one and that he wanted me to leave his house. I looked at my dad in disbelief and didn't understand (not him wanting me to leave, but the ruining of his marriage which had absolutely nothing to do with the kids. It was all the games and lies between he and his wife that they thought no one knew about or was aware of, but we all knew).

I looked at him and said okay and said to him, "You ruined one marriage and not about to ruin another one, so when did you get married again?" and walked out of the kitchen. He asked me when was I going to leave and I told him that I would let him know. I had just paid him rent and bought all food that was in the house that everyone ate; his live-in girlfriend had no job, a cocaine habit, and a son who I dropped off at the subway every morning on my way to work as he attended school.

I got up at 5:00 a.m. on Monday morning. I was furious with my dad as well as heartbroken, called my job, and informed my supervisor that I had an emergency and wouldn't be in for work. I packed everything and moved in with my oldest sister. My dad called my sister and asked her how I was doing. I had absolutely nothing to say to my dad for a few years. One year later, my dad lost everything (his house, his business with my uncle, and his relationships with his family as they all knew what happened and what he had done to me and why).

Months went by and my sister and I could no longer afford the uptown apartment and take care of our kids. We moved to a cheaper apartment in Washington DC. In scoping out the neighborhood, I took my son out for a walk and noticed a young man who kept staring at me and as I looked at him, our eyes locked, we spoke, exchanged a few words as well as exchanged phone numbers.

A few days later, he called me. We talked and decided to see each other. We started seeing each other as well as spending a lot of time together. I knew he had a girlfriend and I really didn't care. One morning, at 2:00 a.m., there was a loud bang on my door. I jumped up, went to the door, and said, "Who is it?" It was one of his buddies telling me that he was outside in front of my building, lying on the ground, and calling my name and that the paramedics were trying to revive him from being shot several times.

He was taken to the nearest hospital, operated on and placed in the intensive care unit. I received a phone call from his father in which I had met several weeks earlier as he wanted to show his dad where he spent most of his time in the neighborhood. His dad called me and asked if I wanted to go to the hospital to see him. I said yes and he picked me up later that evening. As we were riding to the hospital, his dad told me that he had seen me a couple of times outside with my son, and asked if I was dating his son and if so, did I love him. I looked at his dad and told him that his son and I had been seeing each other. I didn't love his son, but I did care about him and that I also knew that his son had a girlfriend. When we got to the hospital and entered the hospital room, there he laid in the hospital bed with his girlfriend by his side. His dad and I looked at each other and smiled, wondering where was she when all this was going on.

Upon leaving the hospital and riding home, my friend's dad proceeded to let me know that he had been watching me whenever he saw me in the neighborhood with my son, and that the Lord told him that I was his wife. I informed him that the Lord might have told him that, but the Lord sure didn't share that one with me. We decided to start seeing each other, talked on the phone until the sun came up; we talked about anything and everything as the friendship and love grew deeper and deeper without romance or sex.

Three weeks later, upon my friend and his son's return home from the hospital, his dad informed me that he was going to have a talk with his son to let him know that we were dating and that whatever was between myself and his son was now and officially over. I agreed. As his son needed a ride home from the hospital to his mother's house, his dad and I went together to pick him up. His son and I were in the vehicle alone; I asked him if he had a problem with his dad and I dating. He looked at me and said no and you know I have a girlfriend. And I left it at that, only to find out a few weeks later that he told a friend that he was going to leave his girlfriend because he really wanted to be with me.

After several months of seeing each other on a daily basis, dating, eating out, walks in the park on beautiful summer nights, weekend trips to the beach, doing and sharing everything as one, and showing great interest, and spending most of his time with my son, and my son wanting to spend his time with him as well, showing and teaching him things as a father would a son, made him more attractive, and I certainly knew without a shadow of a doubt that I loved this man and he was what I had been praying and asking God for. I decided it was time for me to move out from under my sister and that I had to stop moving back and forth from relative to relative and build a life and solid foundation for my son and myself. It was time for me to be a true woman and mother, take responsibility, and be held accountable for the woman and mother that I was.

I prayed and God led me to an apartment that I could afford in a nice neighborhood. A childhood friend of mine worked for the realtor company who owned the apartment complex and lived on the property as well (won't God do it). I obtained the keys to my new apartment, and to my surprise, my friend told me to stay home and relax for the day. He had hired and paid a moving company to move our (my son and myself) belongings into my new place, decorated the apartment, stocked the cabinets, refrigerator, and freezer with food and drinks. He took my son with him for the day; he stated that he wanted to start showing him things that a man should do, a man should handle for his woman, and how to be a gentleman and from that day forward, we were never apart. The family bond and foundation with the three of us became stronger and stronger as we both agreed that we would never allow anything or anyone to come in between us and the no man would take asunder.

Seven years went by, as we attempted to have additional children and nothing happened. Just when I said, "Okay, God, I am okay with one child," and came into acceptance that we may only have that one child. Several weeks later, I became constantly tired, sick most of the time, and slept most of the evening. He had taken a night job to ensure that one of use were always home with our son. I asked him to stop and bring me a pregnancy test before he went to work that evening and as he did, took the test and found I was pregnant. On October 29, 1999, we were blessed with another beautiful son.

Eleven months went by and I became pregnant again, and on December 26, 2000, we had another beautiful son. I thought that was it, and eleven months later, I became pregnant again and decided that I didn't want any more kids and had an abortion. My man was extremely heartbroken and refused to take part in any of it. He didn't speak to me for weeks. I thought that things would go back to normal, until one night, I went to bed and the Lord came to me in a dream and reminded me of the abortion. In my dream, I was laying on the grass (beautiful green pastures) and a minister in a purple robe with gold trimming came to me and said, "The next child that you become pregnant with, do not get an abortion and you will be granted the desires of your heart." I woke up in a sweat and looked over at my man sleeping in the bed and asked God what he meant. I laid back down, went back to sleep. As I was in a deep sleep, God woke me up. I opened my eyes and turned my head toward the door and looked at the side of my bed. I saw an angel kneeling down at the bed and he was so white, bright, and beautiful that the angel had an aura of blue around him.

I closed my eyes, opened them again, and the angel was gone. I turned and looked at my man lying in the bed and the Lord clearly spoke to me and said, "I have sent this man to you as a protector, but you both are living in sin as we were living together and not married."

The Lord also spoke to me and said that your bed is defiled and I am no part of this sinful nature. My heart started pounding as I was sore afraid *of what the* Lord had said as he said it in a *stern* voice. My man had been asking me to marry him for four years, and I kept stating that I was not ready for marriage but had three kids.

The following day, I kept thinking about the dream and what the Lord had said to me. I called my mom and told her that he kept asking me to marry him and told her that I wasn't ready for marriage. My mother always being the realist and always keeping it real and being brutally honest with me and my sisters as we always called her the reality checker, stated to me and these were her exact words, "You have already had babies by him, what else is there to do and you are stuck with him for the rest of your life anyway, so you might as well marry the man and stop making my grandkids bastards." I continued to think about and ponder on the dream, what the Lord said to me and now what my mother said.

Later that night, my man left for work and my oldest son was in his room playing on his Playstation. I had come home from work and had taken a nap and had just taken my youngest son from the other side of my bed and placed him in his crib as he slept and was taking a nap as well. The LORD woke me up as I was in a deep sleep; I looked on the other side of my bed and noticed that my bed was on fire. I woke up and kept patting the bed and fire as it was semi small but growing into a bigger fire. I was able to put the fire out, got up off of the bed and just kept looking at the burn spot in my mattress in disbelief that my bed had actually caught fire. I got up and went into my son's bedroom; he had just turned seven, and I asked him had he been playing with matches and he looked at me as if I was crazy. I went back into my bedroom, looked at my son in his crib, and realized where the fire was is the same spot that my son was laying in before the Lord had me pick him up and place him in his crib which is something that I normally would not have done as I would have allowed him to sleep in my bed. I sat on the bed in disbelief again and the Lord said to me, your bed is a burning bed and it is defiled (the halogen lamp by the bed, the bulb overheated, popped, and fell on my bed). I changed the sheets and comforter, prayed, fed the kids, and we all went to bed for the night.

The next morning as my man had come home from work, tired, and sleepy as I fixed breakfast for him and the kids before I left for work, and my oldest son left for school. I told him what had happened and he just looked at me and said, "Now what?"

I got to work and my supervisor called me in her office (I was working for the property management company where I lived and loved it as I had left my government job with no regrets). She said, "Have a seat." I sat down and she looked at me and said, "I don't know but I am going to tell you what God told me to tell you and God told me to tell you to get your house in order."

I looked at her and sat there with my mouth opened for about two to three minutes, and I knew exactly why God told her to tell me that and I knew exactly what I needed and had to do. The next morning, I called my job and told my supervisor that I had to take off. I had something to do. She asked no questions; we both laughed because of the conversation we had the day before and she said okay and I hung up. As my man was lying in the bed, asleep from a hard night's work, I woke him up and said, "If you want to get married, come on and let's go to the Justice of the Peace before I change my mind."

We got up, got dressed, and with the two youngest kids in tow, and went to the justice of the peace and got married (we had done blood work and test months beforehand).

4

The Intervention

"I Love the Lord" by Whitney Houston
"Different" by Tasha Page Lockhart
"Let Your Power Fall" by James Fortune & FIYA (featuring Zacardi Cortez)

> Throw me to the wolves and I will return leading the pack.
>
> —Seneca

> A strong woman looks a challenge in the eye and gives it a wink.
>
> —Gina Carey

> A woman is like a tea bag; you never know how strong she is until she gets in hot water.
>
> —Eleanor Roosevelt

> At the end of the day, I'm at peace because my intentions are good and my heart is pure.
>
> —Power of Positivity

The Lord said: "For he is no longer your concern. For I have taken him now. Forgive him, for he doesn't understand what he has done. For he is now in my hands and there is nothing else you can do for him. For what you think and know that the canker worm has taken from you, for I (the Lord) will return to you one-hundred fold. Handle my (God) business and I (God) will handle yours for he is now in my hands. The platform has been set. Follow my instructions and hold on to my unchanging hand. For you have been hand-picked and hand chosen by me and me alone. They don't understand me (God); therefore, they don't understand you."

Two years passed and three children later, we decided that we needed a bigger place to live as our family had grown as we moved into a bigger apartment one month later. I started feeling tired, sick, and sleepy most of the time and didn't need a pregnancy test as I knew I was pregnant and on August 21, 2002, we had a beautiful daughter.

My daughter had just turned two years old, and we had gone out for the day to celebrate her birthday, and when we got home everyone was exhausted from the day filled with fun, games, laughter, and plenty of food. We gave the kids a bath and put them to bed. Once all the kids were asleep, my husband and I decided to have a glass of wine and good conversation to end the night as we had a great day, all of the kids were healthy, strong, and happy. Once in the bed, I fell asleep and the Lord gave me a dream and spoke to me and in the dream, I was in the bed and surrounded by plenty of raw eggs and bowls, and I saw a young girl slumped over the bed backward with her head rolling back and forth and I proceeded to crack the eggs and separate the yolks from the egg whites, and the Lord said I have given you the power to cast out demons and break yolks. I woke up and thought about the dream, asked God what does this dream mean and I went back to sleep. A couple of days later, I was cleaning up the house, playing my gospel music and the kids were in the room playing. I started singing "I Go to the Rock" that was playing by Whitney Houston, and I was leaning down and couldn't get up and the Lord said to me again in a *stern* voice, I have given you power to cast out demons, and once he spoke it, I stood up, sat on the couch in the living room, and said, "Okay God, I heard you." All of a sudden, one of the kids came out of the room, calling my name, I went in the room, and one of the kids had been acting up and misbehaving all day long. I looked at my child and backed up from what I saw. I was afraid at first. I told the other kids to go in the room. I scooped my child up in my arms and started praying and quoting what the Lord said as my child continued to yell and scream and say, "Don't say that to me," as I was praying in the name of Jesus, and my child continued to scream, "Don't lay hands on me. I don't want you to do that!" in a voice that I had never heard before. I went into my bedroom, laid my child on the bed, and continued to pray, and now with the power and authority that the Lord told me that he had given me. After taking the power and authority that the Lord had given me and using it, I picked my child up, continued to pray, and cast out and my child slumped in my arms and started to weep in a childlike manner. I held my child in my arms and kept praying in the name of Jesus and knew when the demon had departed. I then went in the bathroom, got a rag, and wet it, wiped my child down, tied the rag up, and placed it in the trash. I took the trash outside to the dumpster. I prayed, told the thing to get out of my house, and that it was no longer allowed to reside. I washed my hands and face as the kids started playing, dancing and talking as if nothing ever happened. As I sat on the couch in awe of what had just taken place and said, "God, that's what you were talking about and he said again, I have given you the power and authority to cast out demons." And I just looked up and just thought about the wonderful and amazing God I serve and how God will give you exactly what you need and more, even if sometimes we don't deserve it, or we don't realize what it is that we need.

A couple of years had passed and I was released from my position at the property management company where I had worked for seven years (seven being the number of completion). I had been thinking about the medical field for a year or so, sent out several resumés to other organizations and not the medical field, only for me to have all of the resumés returned to me, saying returned to sender for additional postage and knowing that it only took one stamp to send a two page resumé. I heard the Lord say, "Once I equip you, only then will I send you back out amongst the wolves." Not knowing what that meant, I said, "Okay, Lord."

Later that night, the Lord gave me a dream and we had just started going to the church where my family and I had just become members. In my dream, my pastor was in my home in a white suit and said follow me, the Lord wants me to take you somewhere, and as I followed, the path led to a low, deep, and dark place, and when I turned to look and ask my pastor where we were going, he was gone. I continued to walk and ended up in a hospital with green and white walls and walked into an office where people were pulling and tugging at each other, trying to scratch each other's eyes out and as I turned to ask the Lord, "What do I do?" I woke up. Two weeks later, I went to the local hospital, filled out an application, and left. One week went by, and I received a phone call from the hospital, requesting me to come in for an interview. I went for the interview several days later as the Lord told me once I finished the interview and was on my way to my vehicle that the job was mine.

A month went past, and I was in the house by myself cleaning and heard nothing from the organization for which I had applied and interviewed. I said to the Lord, "Lord, I thought I knew you and I thought you told me that the job was mine and left it at that." I had just received my last unemployment check the week before, and my husband was working as much overtime as he could to make ends meet. As I was playing music and was coming into my bedroom, I noticed that the answering machine light was blinking. I had not heard the phone ring, I sat on the bed, listened to the message, and it was the medical facility department director informing me that she had chosen me for the position and wanted to know when I could start. I praised God, called her back, and we confirmed that I would start in one week on a Monday. I forgot that we didn't have the money to pay the phone bill and as soon as I hung up from the medical facility and confirming my start date, I went to the phone to page my husband to tell him the good news. The phone was dead and realized that the phone had been disconnected. Once again, God allowed me to get what I needed to get done.

I started working at the medical facility in which I loved. As my husband was taking me to work on a bright and sunny morning as he had just gotten off from his night job and kept telling me that he didn't feel too good and that he was going home and lay down. After dropping me off at work, a couple of hours later, he called me and told me that he didn't think he was going to make it or going to live as his chest was in excruciating pain. He was taken to the hospital and to find that he had a massive heart attack. He was placed in the critical care unit as we didn't know if he was going to make it (but God). I called my pastor later that night around midnight, and we began to pray. The next morning, I went to the hospital and the nurse that was caring for him, who was not a believer, looked at me and said that they had to give him a couple of shots as his heart almost stopped beating several times, and she stated, "All of a sudden, everything started turning around."

I asked her, "What time was it?" and she stated around 1am (that was the same time we were praying), I looked at her and chuckled and said, "Look at God." Several days later, my husband being a vet, was transferred to the Veterans Administration Hospital and was discharged seven days later (seven being the number of completion) and came home healthy and strong.

Two years passed and once again we decided that we needed a bigger place and God blessed us with a townhome. My husband started having back pain, went to the doctors, and was informed that he had herniated disks in his back and needed to have surgery. He pondered on the decision as he decided to have the surgery. Several weeks later, as we traveled to Baltimore, the surgery took place and seemed to be successful. My employer allowed me to go visit my husband in Baltimore during the day and work at night as I would go home after visiting with him, be home when the kids got home from school, cooked dinner, helped with homework, and then headed to work for eight hours. The day that my husband was to be released from the hospital, I received a phone call from the medical facility informing me that my husband had to be rushed back into surgery as they noticed that upon him going to therapy that day before being released, that he had a spinal fluid leak. I rushed to Baltimore, and there he lay on his side, as the doctors informed him not to move. If he did move, it could lead to being brain dead, brain damage, or paralysis. He had to lay, eat, sleep, and use the bathroom on his side for seven days (again seven being the number of completion). On the eighth day, he was released from the hospital and told me that he didn't think he was going to live (but God).

Several years passed and things started to get rough financially, and we moved into an apartment. I thanked God for a place to live, and I dreaded the neighborhood, but God had a plan for my life. We lived there for one year.

My husband had a doctor's appointment and was informed that they wanted to run test as we both agreed. One week later, his doctor called and said that he needed for us to come in and that he needed to discuss a few things with us. My husband was nervous and afraid and so was I. Two days later, we went to the doctor's office and as we sat in anticipation, waiting for the doctor to enter the room, he entered as we all stood, and he went over the test results and informed my husband and myself that my husband had been diagnosed with prostate cancer and that it was at the highest level, PSA of 9, which we found out was very high, and he needed to start treatment. My husband's knees buckled and the doctor explained that prostate cancer is a slow growing cancer and can be cured and that we would hope for the best. As we drove home in complete silence, I prayed for several months. My husband didn't want to talk about or discuss the diagnosis or treatment. My first lady and I continued to pray and I kept seeing cancer treatment commercials on television for a month straight every night while watching television.

Several weeks later, as I was sitting at work, I received a phone call from a young lady, and she informed me that my husband had just called her as she was from a cancer treatment center and that he wanted to come in and be screened to see if he was a candidate for treatment. Several weeks later, arrangements were made as one of my church members and a very dear person to my heart who is like an aunt to me, drove us to the treatment center and kept the kids for a week. We found that he was a candidate, they took the insurance that we had and treatment would start in two weeks. We returned home to prepare for the treatment as my husband had to stay at the treatment center for three months.

After three months of treatment, great staff who cared, and a great facility, my husband came home cancer free (look at God) with a PSA of 0.1. He had been cancer free from that point on. Things were looking up and we were blessed with a beautiful home in Fort Washington, Maryland, where everyone had their own room, and we were blessed financially where we could afford everything that we needed and most of what we wanted.

Two years passed, and my husband was diagnosed with kidney failure, and we were informed that he would have to have dialysis three times a week. My husband and I talked and talked and talked about it, and finally a month later, he agreed. He started dialysis treatment in which he became sicker and sicker and had more frequent hospital stays; sometimes a month at a time. Only to come home at 6:00 p.m. and I would have to call 911 two hours later, and he would have to go back in the hospital for weeks at a time. As this continued for a year and a half, the kids saw their dad sick and suffering, with the ambulance at the house frequently to where after a while, it became the norm for us all. As my husband became frustrated and angry from being sick on a constant basis, he became very irritable and angry. I knew that it wasn't him; it was the sickness that tried to control him, his mind, and spirit.

One month later, my husband was out fairly late at night. He had not done that in years and called and informed me that he was taking one of his friends' girlfriend to see him as he was incarcerated, and he would be home a little later on. I didn't think anything of it and said okay. As it was going on eleven o'clock at night, something in my spirit wasn't sitting right, and I called him in which I never did when he was out or away from the house. He answered the phone as if he was sleep and I asked him, "Where are you, what are you doing and why do you sound like your are sleep?"

He answered and said, "Oh we are watching *Empire* and just go back." I asked him, "How are you watching *Empire* when it's eleven o'clock and *Empire* comes on at ten?" The other end of the phone got silent, and I said, "Oh, okay, so it's like that," and hung up the phone.

You would think that he would come home right away. Instead he came home one and a half hours later 12:30 a.m., and I opened my eyes, looked at the clock, looked at him, said nothing, rolled over in the bed, and went back to sleep.

Two weeks later, my husband called me at work and asked me is there any possibility that he could be burning from the flu shot that he received. I asked him burning from the front or the back, and he stated the back (I knew he was not being truthful). I hung up the phone and continued to work at my desk. Later that night, we were lying in bed, watching a movie, and he informed me that he had gone to the doctor earlier in the day and that the doctor informed him that what he had, he needed to go the emergency room and get a shot as she could not cure what he had in the office.

I looked at him and said, "Well don't lay here in the bed with me, when you need to go to the ER and get cured." We had not been intimate for quite some time as I had no desire to be intimate with him by any means as he always desired intimacy from and with me.

He got up and went to the emergency room. He came home at 2:00 a.m. that morning and tried to show me the discharge papers and tried to explain the diagnosis. I did not want to see nor hear about it, I already knew what was going on. I looked at him and said, "Oh the woman you were with burned you, huh."

He tried to start an argument, which I refused to do, and it made no sense, because at that point, I was done, done with him and done with the marriage in which I had been distant from and not into for quite some time—for several years as a matter of fact (I had never and would never cheat as I valued my relationship, commitment to God, marriage, my husband, and family too much).

As a woman of God, lady, wife, and mother, I continued to be a wife to my husband, no matter what the circumstances were. I continued to cook, serve him his food, fix him breakfast in the morning, and prepared his lunch before I left for work on a daily basis (I would and will not allow anyone else's behavior or actions, define who and who's I am, the woman of God, the wife, and mother that I became). I continually asked God if I could leave my marriage. He never answered me, so I knew that I could not go anywhere or do anything without God's direction, leading, or guiding.

One week later, as I was getting out of my vehicle to go to work, I fell on the ice and I saw my wrist go limp. Working in a medical facility, I went to the emergency room, only to find that I had broken my right wrist in two places and had to be off work for several months (God knew what he was doing and had a plan for my life). I believe God was preparing me for the death of my husband and knew that I needed more than one week of bereavement leave, and I ended up being off work for three months on workman's compensation.

Two weeks went by and I noticed that my husband had not been to dialysis all week, and as he attempted to break into the real estate business, real estate had become his priority as opposed to his health. One night as we laid in the bed, my husband jumped up and went into the bathroom where he stayed for an hour. I got up out of the bed and told him to open the door. He opened the door, I could see the fluid buildup in his face. He didn't want me to know that he was sitting on the commode trying to sleep and he could not lie in the bed due to the fluid buildup. The next morning came, and he got dressed and stated that he was headed to real estate class. I could see that he wasn't feeling well at all. I informed him not to come back to the house after class, but to go to the emergency room and have them check him out as I could see the fluid in his body building and to see him that way was not fair to the kids, me, or himself and that he needed to go to the hospital immediately.

Several hours later, my husband called me from the emergency room and informed me that they were admitting him immediately and that he was certainly on fluid overload and had to be dialyzed right away. I got up, went to the hospital as he had to be placed in the intensive care unit and had to be dialyzed daily for a week. Three days later, the kids and I went to the hospital as he was placed on another floor (a step down unit) where everything seemed to be fine as we all discussed what we were going to do and how we would eat healthier upon his return home. Two days passed, and I received a phone call, informing me that my husband had been taken back to ICU. I arrived at the hospital with the kids as they stated that they wanted to see their dad. I told them, "Let me go first because we don't know what is going on." They wanted to see their dad as I didn't refuse them, only to walk into the ICU unit, and to see him lethargic, foaming at the mouth, and screaming from the pain. My kids were devastated and crying. I told them to go back to the truck; I would be there in a bit. I talked to the hospital staff and told them to clean my husband up as we should not have come in and saw him this way. I returned to the vehicle, talked to the kids, and they seemed a little better as they were used to him being in the hospital and always pulling through and coming home.

The next morning, as I laid in the bed trying to rest and in pain from my wrist being broken, I heard bells ringing and noticed that the dogs didn't bark as they always did if they heard any type of noise. I got up and went to the door as no one was there. I lay back on the bed and said, "Okay, God, are you opening the windows of heaven?" The next day, as I hadn't eaten in two days, I went to the hospital *as* my husband was on a ventilator and seemed to be resting peacefully. I walked into the room and it was just he and I; I kissed him on his face, rubbed his forehead, and proceeded to have a conversation with him. I said to him, "Honey, we have had a good run and life together, we have had some good times and bad times, I have gotten on your nerves and Lord knows you have gotten on mine. We have four beautiful children and have a strong relationship and foundation with God and I know you are tired and it's okay now. It's truly okay and I understand." I told my husband, "You do what you feel you have to do and whatever you choose to do. It is truly okay, I love you and I know you love me and what we have had for twenty-five years, many people have never had in their entire life."

I gave him another kiss, told him to rest now, and walked out of the room. I knew in my spirit a week beforehand that he wasn't coming home, and I never shared what I knew with anyone.

As I walked out of the hospital at 7:00 p.m., the sun was shining, and there was a mist, and sprinkle shower of rain that was so beautiful, I looked up at the sky and said, "Okay, God, now you are commencing the spirit up to heaven, and thinking that I would have at least another week or so with my husband." I went home, ate a really good meal and was going to lay down and watch television as the kids were home from school and everyone was asleep.

One hour later, at 8:00 p.m., the phone rang, I looked at the caller ID, and it was the hospital. I looked at the phone again and said, "Lord, please don't do this today," and to give me more time and as I answered the phone, the doctor was on the other end and informed me that they had been working on my husband for the last hour and that he had gone into cardiac arrest five times. He stated the he didn't know if my husband's heart could take anymore and it was humanly unfair as to what they were doing. All I heard him say was, "He's coding again, I gotta go." The doctor called me back ten minutes later and stated that he had pronounced my husband dead five minutes ago. My first thought was, *How am I going to tell my kids that their father is gone?* And I froze.

5

The Healing

"Break Every Chain" by Tasha Cobbs
"Never Be Bound Again" by Bishop Paul Morton
"You Have Won the Victory" by Full Gospel Baptist Church

> When a woman knows what she brings to the table, she is not afraid to eat alone.
>
> —Entity

#HER

> Her grind is serious and her faith is unimaginable, her swag flawless. Most people are fooled by her pretty face, but this queen can hold her own and some. She knows how to handle her business. Life experiences taught her who to keep in her court and while she may seem too much for a joker…she is perfect for a king.
>
> —Pierre Alex Jeanty

> There's something about a woman with a loud mind that sits in silence, smiling, knowing she can crush you with the truth (r.g. moon)

A strong woman will automatically stop trying if she feels unwanted. She won't fix it or beg; she'll just walk away.

—Power of Positivity

You may forget what someone said. You may forget what someone did. You will never forget how someone made you feel. (Maya Angelou)

On October 17,2017, God said to me, "Healing is taking place in you, for it will soon be finished and those that have hurt and betrayed you will need your prayers and help and you will do the work. You will be the only one that they can turn to, for I (God) will make it that way. They will be hesitant to come to you and will have no other choice. To you I (God) say, touch not the unclean thing and again, say nothing when you know that they are talking, for I (the Lord) will elevate you. Keep your lines of communication open for the mouth of the Lord has spoken. For I the Lord say, they do not know that their own demise has come and is set for an appointed time. Touch not my anointed and do my prophet no harm. Praise me in advance for this thing is done."

Once I snapped out of being in shock from the news that my husband was now deceased, I called my oldest son as he rushed from work to comfort and assist me and told me to go to the hospital and do what I needed to do. My step son and I went to the hospital. He was the only one from my husband's side of the family who was there for me until the end. As we walked into the room where my husband's body lay, his skin was shining like the sun, his eyes were looking straight up toward the sky, and he had the biggest smile on his face, and at that point I knew he was ready to go, and he was at peace with God and himself.

I knew that I had been a good wife, mother, caretaker, confidant, and friend to my husband and that was one thing that no one could take away from me. The Lord had been preparing me for the last three years as I handled everything concerning myself and my family (bills, finances, work, household issues and concerns, kids, after-school activities, school, and all medical decisions, information and responsibilities concerning my husband).

As I entered the house from viewing my husband's body, my two sons took on the task of telling my next to the oldest son and my daughter (who is the youngest of all) that their dad passed away and to see the tears and pain in their eyes and the devastation on their faces as they were always used to their dad pulling through and returning home from a hospital stay, was a hurt and a heartbreak that I never wanted to endure and wouldn't wish on my worst enemy.

I decided to tell my middle son, who was very close to his dad. I woke him with a soft touch to his cheek, and as he woke, I just looked at him as he returned the look and said, "What is it, Ma?" I looked him in the eyes and told him that his dad had just passed away. My son buried his face in his pillow as he wept and wept and wept. I lifted him up, held him in my arms, and rocked him back and forth as I could feel his pain and I wished I could take the pain away from all of my children and take it myself as I love my children more than life itself and would lay my life down any day for either one of them. I knew that this would be a process for each one of us and that each of us would handle the grieving and emotional process differently and in our own way. I also knew that I had to prepare as best as I could through much prayer and fasting to assist each of them to be able to get through this process.

Two days after my husband's passing, I was at home, preparing to meet my stepson and go to the funeral home to make funeral arrangements. My husband's cell phone rang, and at that moment, I remembered that I didn't call the cell phone company to have the line turned off. I answered his cell phone and the woman on the other end said hello. I said hello as she went on to explain how she thought she dialed a girlfriend's number. I stopped her in the middle of her forever-going explanation and told her that she was doing a little too much explaining and that if she was calling for my husband (I knew she was), that he had passed away two days ago. There was a dead silence on the other end of the phone. I then in turn said, "I hope you are okay and have a good day," and hung up.

As my children and I arrived at the funeral home to bury my husband and their father, it was a beautiful day and a beautiful home-going service as my kids, myself and my husband's ex-wife all stood that day as a family to honor and celebrate his home going. After the service, we entered the restaurant in which we rented and reserved for the re-pass and after the food was served, I started going from table to table to thank everyone for coming and giving their condolences. I got to a table where there were two women who I didn't recognize nor had I ever met. I knew in my spirit and in my heart which one was the other woman in whom my husband had an affair and knew that it was the woman that I had spoken with on the phone. I greeted the both of them, thanked them for coming; the woman that my husband had and was having an affair with couldn't look at me. I looked at her, tapped her on the arm, and as she struggled to look me in the face, I thanked her for coming and sharing in the home-going service for my husband and my children's father and that I hoped that they enjoyed the food, informed them that there was plenty of food left, and to help themselves to as much food as they wanted. I looked at her, smiled, turned, and walked away.

I knew that God was doing a work in me as well as healing and intervention was taking place and as I walked away from her, I wasn't mad, bitter, angry, nor felt an ounce of hatred or resentment toward her. I actually felt sorry for her as she couldn't even let the world know who she was or how she felt about my husband. I could see the hurt in her eyes when she finally was able to look at me, as in God's eyes, he didn't belong to her, he belonged to God, my kids, and I.

Once I got home and thought about it, I chuckled and wondered where was she when I had to deal with all the hospital stays, medical scares, cancer treatments, and running up and down the road for weeks at a time after work, school, homework with the kids, dinner, and being in school myself to earn my degree and to ensure that my husband was being taken care of properly, professionally, and medically. Where was she when the lengthy discussions had to take place with teams of physicians and specialists regarding his health issues and final analysis and outcomes which could, would, and did end in death? After thinking about it and his affair, I wouldn't have done it or handled him, his health issues, nor love that I had for him any other way. He was always a great father to his children, a good husband who supported me in everything I did or decided to do good, bad, or indifferent. A man who was still my friend that I could talk to about anything and share anything with without judgment. A man who knew my inner most secrets, heartaches, heart breaks, hurts, disappointments, loves, and losses, and a man who, even through his affair, I never once ever doubted his love for me. I knew he loved me with all his heart and soul in which he often told me so. A man who wasn't afraid to show me his vulnerabilities, hurts, tears, fears, and certainly was never afraid or embarrassed or didn't feel like he wasn't a man because of how much he loved me and was never afraid or embarrassed to show or tell others that I was the love of his life.

God dealt with my husband and his affair in his own way as my husband often shared with me that he was afraid that I was going to leave him. I realized that it was not for me to neither judge my husband nor punish him for what he did as we are all human; none of us are perfect, and we all make mistakes. His fault and affair were openly exposed and I was not his judge. God is the judge and judger of all and that is God's title alone, not mine. Realizing what I had with my husband of twenty-five years, some people have never had in their entire life, and for that, to God and my husband; I am truly blessed and sincerely grateful for the marriage, relationship, and friendship that I shared with him.

Several months after my husband's death and burial, I re-connected with my first love and who I had not seen or run into for over twenty years. Once we texted and messaged for a day and a half, he wanted to talk on the phone. We did and decided to see each other. We saw each other and it was like old times as we laughed, ate, and talked, and it felt as if we had never lost touch with each other. A month or so went by as we were always together or talking on the phone. I thought that the person that I once loved dearly and was once in love with would have my back through one of the most difficult times in my life, and I thought would truly understand me and what I was going through if no one else did. Only to find out and as time went by that instead of being happy for me with my life's accomplishments, achievements, progression, and four beautiful children, who he never met, except for my oldest by accident. Instead it was jealousy and bitterness. I couldn't understand why he would always come to my house and just look around at what my husband and I had built together and would just sit and stare at me. I didn't pay it much attention at the time, being that I am not and have never been a jealous or envious person and didn't quite understand how jealousy worked or could be so treacherous, detrimental, and dangerous. My dad always taught me that you can have just as much as the next person, if not more. You have to work for what you want, make your word your bond (sometimes that's all you have is your word), and always be honest and true to and with yourself and who you are.

Several months went by and as my kids were with their brother for the summer in which they had never stayed away from me or home that long. I thought that it was a blessing that I had that time alone and for that long (the devil thought he had me, tried to set a trap and tried to kill me, but God). I started to notice the snappy comments and stares from my friend such as looking me up and down and basically gritting on me, stating comments such as "Not only do you have a good job, you make good money," and standing in my home, just looking around and staring, going through my cabinets and pantry in the middle of the night to see how much food I had as I always believed in keeping my home stocked with plenty of food and drinks. When we were together, I would wake up in the middle of the night and would see him just staring at me as I slept. Then comments such as, "I don't know what's wrong with me, I am crazy."

When someone shows you who they are, *believe them!* Then came the nights when I wouldn't hear from him at all and didn't realize that he had the same gambling habit that he had when we were together over twenty years ago; it had gotten ten times worse. In realizing what he was doing, I then knew that it was time for me to relinquish him, the gambling habits, and the other women that he thought that I didn't know about (I cared about him, but I *loved* me more than I cared about him). One Friday night, he and I had a two-hour phone conversation and decided to see each other the next day. I tried reaching him on several occasions the next day as he texted me back with a lame excuse, and at that point, I knew that he couldn't face me or tell me what happened as I knew that he had gone to the casino the night before and gambled away all his money. I never talked to him again and was extremely hurt in the beginning and not because of the ceased communication, but hurt because of the person who I once loved and cared so deeply for, betrayed me (It wasn't him that did it, God did it, and today, I know that God knew exactly what he was doing and I'm glad God did it that way).

Several months later, a friend of mine whom I used to work with went to Africa and brought back gifts and wanted to have lunch and make a girls day of it. I agreed and was happy to do so. Only for us to walk into the restaurant and to my surprise, I looked, stepped back, stepped forward, and looked again, and lo and behold, it was the guy who completely went ghost, sitting in the restaurant, eating with another woman and stabbing at the food as if he were starving and hadn't eaten in weeks. I ever so kindly looked at him as the hostess of the restaurant escorted my friend and me to our table, smiled, and kept going. At that point, I knew that I was over it, over him, and the situation. A person of that nature and character (in which he had none) was no good for me and was more toxic to himself, than toxic to me. His gambling habits and lies were a strong hold; I realized that many demons lay inside of him and this is a person that I laid beside many nights (I was truly sleeping with the enemy and didn't even know that he truly hated me and I believe was on get-back time from the past as he stated that I had hurt him in our past relationship).

A month after seeing my ex in the restaurant, I stopped at the gas station up the street from where I lived one night and was on my way home from work and saw his car just sitting there, beside mine at the gas pump. I shook my head as at that point, he no longer existed to me, and I actually thought it was quite immature and childish to play games as we were now in our fifties. I noticed the dogs would run to the door at 2:00 and 3:00 a.m., barking and growling and just watching the door, walking around the house, sniffing, as they knew his scent and my dogs truly didn't like him. As one of my dogs, after meeting and seeing him for the first time, bit him on his foot. I should have realized then that something wasn't right about him after all these years.

I knew that he would ride past my house or sit outside in my neighborhood around the corner as he had done in the past. I would go outside the house, heading to work in the morning, only to notice and find dents in my truck. I started my truck one morning and it cut off and wouldn't start (I knew then, he had done it). I called my friend, told him about my vehicle, and him being the true gentleman and man of God that he is (not because of what he does for me, because of who he is and who he has been to me) had my vehicle towed to his shop, fixed with no questions asked, and when I seemed to be upset about my vehicle, his response was, "Don't worry about anything, you know how you and I are, and we always make it do what it do, and we are going to be all right, cause God is good." During the time that my vehicle was being repaired, this wonderful man and true friend would adjust his schedule and day, pick me up in the morning, take me to work, and call me at the end of his hard day's work to inform me of what time he would pick me up and take me home as well as anywhere else I needed to go. What a friend and what a man.

Several weeks later, I received a phone call from my mother and as we were holding a conversation, she asked me to allow my sister to come and live with me. My sister had been extremely ill and was going through some of the same illnesses and treatments that my husband had gone through before his passing. I thought about it, prayed about it, pondered on it, and couldn't allow myself to go through what I had just gone through with my husband three months earlier. I responded to my mother and told her that I couldn't do it, and that I was going through my own things at the moment (just burying my husband and still getting his affairs in order, raising three teenagers on my own and by myself, running a household, bills, two dogs, and a demanding career and job). My mother's response to me was, "What could you possibly be going through; I'm disappointed in you and hung up the phone."

I froze in place, my mouth dropped; I couldn't believe what my mother had just said to me after just burying my husband. For several months, I no longer heard from my mother or my sisters. I knew that everyone was upset and talking about the situation; no one called or asked me how I was doing, asked if I needed anything, were the kids okay, or if I needed for them to do anything for me (and that was family).

6

The Deliverance

"You Are God Alone" by Marvin Sapp
"I Don't Mind Waiting on the Lord" by Juanita Bynum
"You Covered Me" by Dr. R.A. Vernon & "The Word" Church
Praise Team led by Tim Reddick

> Sometimes we need to stop analyzing the past, stop planning the future, stop figuring out precisely how we feel, stop deciding exactly what we want, and just see what happens. Let go and let God.
>
> —Carrie Bradshaw

> You may be able to see down the street, God can see down the street, around the corner and knows your final destination. Let God be the pilot of your plane. Get out of the driver's seat, become the passenger, and let God be the pilot, the guide, the director, and the driver of your life.. (Sandra Adona-Durham)

> When you fight to cling to people who are no longer meant to be in your life. You delay your destiny. Let them go. (Mandy Hale)

Often people who criticize your life are the same people that don't know the price you paid to get to where you are today.

—Shannon Alder

If you live for people's acceptance, you'll die from their rejection. (Lecrae)

It's not what I have been through that defines who I am, it's how I got through it that has made me the person I am today.

—Best Quotes for you

God spoke to me and said: "For this is the day when complete healing and deliverance shall take place in you, in all areas of your life. Don't go back, don't go back, don't go back even in temptation don't go back to the old, for I (the Lord) will always have a route of escape for you. Move forward from this day on, don't go back. For I (God) have chosen you for such a time as this and those who have attached themselves to you, see the anointing and calling on your life. They have tried to dim your glow and your light. As of this day, your light and glow will shine better and brighter than ever. He tried to steal, kill and destroy you, but, his plan did not work, don't go back, don't go back. For I (God) know the plans I have for you. I (God) know what's best for you. Your ways are not my ways and your thoughts are not my thoughts, for I am God and I have chosen you for such a time as this. For the mouth of the Lord has spoken."

God started dealing with me, my heart, soul, spirit, and my past regarding truly serving him, forgiveness and self-love (Love God first and loving yourself and others will follow).

One of the many things that God has shown and truly dealt with me with is *forgiveness*. If God forgave me for all that I have done, said, portrayed, and displayed, who am I not to forgive others, especially when someone has done something to me (good, bad, or indifferent). It's easy to love those who love and forgave you. The real test is when you can truly forgive and love those who don't love you, those who talk about you, try to demean your character, your name, take shots, and throw fiery darts at you every chance they get. When you can see, think about, or laugh at someone or people that you know have betrayed you or have done you wrong, or you think about someone or people who have betrayed you or have done injustices to you and you can pray for them, smile when you think about them or even laugh when you think about what they did to you, you are truly onto something and are on the road to true forgiveness, healing, and deliverance.

In knowing what my ex did, the actions that he took and the shots and bricks that he tried to throw at me, I can truly and honestly say and know that I forgive him, I wish him well and pray that God gives him the desires of his heart as well and I pray that he finds a true and genuine relationship with the Lord if he already hasn't.

I think about my past, past relationships, past hurts, past trials and tribulations, past tests, past blessings, and true rewards and gifts from God. As I look back over my life I now know that my past, coupled with my present, has made me the woman of God, the lady, the person, the mother, the career woman, the friend, the encourager, the helper, the sister, and the daughter that I am and the wife that I once was and I can truly say, I love God and I love me. I am proud of who God has made me and who I have become (God is still working on me). I am truly humble, grateful, and truly embedded in God, cradled in his arms, and I rest in his bosom, and I know that God brought me through it and to it all, and how you go through determines where you get to!

God has delivered me from pleasing people and now I look at what pleases him (God). I am no longer concerned about what people say, how they feel, or what they think about me (I may think about it but no longer worried or concerned), because I truly know who and whose I am. I am loving life and have come into loving being a woman of God who makes her own decisions (with God's leading and guidance). I love being single and I love being married. I love being with my children and I love being by myself. I love being able to lay in my bed alone and I love being able to think about being married again and having that special person to share everything with. I love being able to get up and go when I want, and I love having that person to share my day with. All these things coupled together and going through what I have gone through has been a true journey, many life lessons, compromises, and sacrifices, and I can now at this point and time in my life, truly say, I wouldn't change anything that has happened to me or through me because I know God did it and it was set in his divine order. God allowed all that happened and I'm not ashamed or embarrassed by anything that has happened in my life (past or present) as God was in the midst of it all.

I know that I am truly, truly blessed, and I am anointed by God to do all that I do, handle all that I handle, and strengthened by God to endure all that I have endured and endure all that I endure.

I have four beautiful children: a son one who is now grown, a true gentleman, on his own, good job (majored in psychology), his own home, has a relationship with his biological father, knows who he is and is not ashamed of it and was raised in the Word of God. A twenty-year-old son who is now in college (majoring in sports management), a true gentleman who knows what he wants to do, knows what he wants in and out of life, and a true man of God who has a great and high calling on his life.

A nineteen-year-old son who is a true football player (has colleges and coaches looking at him already for football), getting ready for college (majoring in sports medicine), does well in school, a true gentleman, and knows what he wants in and out of life, and is very aware of who he is, what he wants and sets his standards very high and loves the Lord and has a true calling on his life. A seventeen-year-old daughter who knows who she is and not ashamed of it, doesn't allow anyone to tell her just anything, she wants proof, wants to be an Executive Chef, and if you don't want to know, don't ask her because she will tell you and will tell you nothing but the truth (a true replica of her mom), loves the Lord, has a true gift from God, and God was in the midst of it all and they all truly love their mom and their mom truly loves them as motherhood is one of the best things that has ever happened to me.

My relationship with my sisters and my mother has been restored. At one time, we weren't in communication at all. But now, when a decision needs to be made concerning my sister, her health, well-being and/or care, God has made me the one that is called upon for an answer, resolution, or final decision. In making all decisions for my sister, I seek God in all that I do, ask, or think, and wait for an answer as I do all things from the heart. God doesn't allow me to think about what was; God only allows me to think about and make the best decisions concerning her and whatever is best for her and I love her dearly.

In my marriage, I know that I was a good wife, caretaker, friend, and confidant. I am at peace with the way I cared for and loved my husband and the way I handled everything concerning him. I know that my husband is no longer suffering and is in a better place and he is with the Lord and I am truly ready for a new start and ready for the next chapter in my life.

My relationship and friendship with my oldest son's biological father is good; we are able to talk and discuss whatever situation is at hand concerning our son as well as ourselves, what we want out of life and our future. I truly know in my heart that our son was made and created out of love that we have and have always had for one another. I hold no grudge, anger, or bitterness with him, and he holds no grudge, anger, or bitterness with me as we respect each other; actually I look at him as quite an amazing man that I will always love. Even though we never had the relationship that I believe we both wanted and longed for at one point and time in our lives. He is someone who will always be special to me and will always hold a special place and love in my heart that nobody else can touch or hold and can never be compared or measured as God used him and me to create and share an amazing son.

I love my father (rest his soul) and I know that he did the best he could by me as he had been on his own at a very young age. My father became a great entrepreneur and well-respected in his community. My father was certainly no stranger to hard work and making it happen, which is where I get my work ethics, being a hard worker, and knowing that you can have just as much as the next person and even more, you have to work hard, always strive for the best, and I know he always wanted what was best for me.

I love my mother. I know she loves me and has made huge sacrifices for her children as I saw my mother start all over on her own with four girls and made things happen, made it work, and made ends meet. I hold no grudges, no bitterness, no anger, no animosity, and no strife with anyone as I know I wasn't always right and didn't always handle things, people, life, or life situations in the best way. By no means was I or am I perfect, and I know I tried to do the best I could by all who I encountered and all who encountered me.

I now know in my marriage and intimate relationships that God took me from good (my marriage), to bad (my friendship with my ex) and now God is going to truly bring me his best! The next chapter in my life, my children, and my Boaz. The book of Habakkuk 2:1–3, says, "Write the vision and make it plain." I have prayed, talked to God, and asked God for what I want, and I have written it down and made it plain and placed it in my Bible, waiting for the manifestation of God's word and his *will* for my life (Psalm 84:11) "For the Lord God is a sun and shield: the Lord will give grace and glory; no good thing will He withhold from them that walk uprightly." I am waiting on God and no longer trying to make things happen or make it work on my own accord. I can no longer be the pilot as I have now become the passenger on the plane and God is the pilot and the driver of my life. I may be able to see down the street, but God can see down the street, around that corner, and knows the final destination. God knows things I don't know and can see things I cannot see. I am learning to wait on God as he makes no mistakes and knows what I need and what I don't need, even if I think it's what I want (Isaiah 55:8–11): "For my thoughts are not your thoughts, neither are your ways my ways, declares the Lord. As the heavens are higher than the earth, so are my ways higher than yours and my thoughts than your thoughts."

Jeremiah 29:11: "For I know the plans I have for you, declares the Lord, plans to prosper you and not to harm you, plans to give you hope and a future". Who wouldn't serve a God and a father like that! I am truly in a place where life is good, even through all that goes on and through the trials and tribulations that I now face (As I face them all with God). I have true joy and peace (now I know what it means to have true joy and peace that passes all understanding). I love who I am, I love me, who I have become, and even more so, who I am becoming in God and I need no validation, confirmation or acceptance from anyone or anything (only God). I never imagined being in this place of Loving God so much; it's like falling in love for the very first time! Being delivered and healed from all the hurt, heartbreak, betrayals, and bricks that life and people threw at me and still being able to love is a blessing and a true gift from God. I have experienced true love, had true love, and know what true love feels like and what it is. I know the happiness, hurts, joy, and sacrifices of love, and I am not afraid of it because I have had it to the fullest and the love that I have had, have experienced, and the true love that I have with God, some people have never experienced or had in their entire life and once again, I am truly blessed and grateful for it.

We as a people often hear that we need to be healed, delivered, and set free from what has us bound, tied up, shackled, and are often not informed or instructed of how it should be done for us to be set free from what has us this way. Speaking for myself and many can relate, being healed and delivered from something(s) that has you bound, tied up, bitter, angry, and hateful. You first have to recognize what it is, be honest with God and yourself, and stop being in denial and admit that you have issues and know that you need help. If you know it's something and you are not sure what it is, ask God and the Holy Spirit to show you the error of your ways, show you what it is, and stop blaming everything and everyone else for the way that you are and the way that your life has turned out and become, as only God is the only one who can truly deliver and heal you from yourself, from the hurt and pain that you have endured and are holding onto. Many of us are not even aware of the childhood templates (things that have happened to you as a young child, teenager or young adult) that have and are affecting your life, relationships, and even mar-riage. You believe and think that you are ok and truly you aren't and you have to be honest, admit that you are a mess (as we all are with-out God) and know that only God can change you, your heart and you have to make the choice to open yourself up, open your heart and accept God's help, healing and deliverance. God will not force anything upon us as God will move on to the next person who truly wants it, will accept and receive it. Once you open up, call, and cry out to God, take God at his word, accept, receive, hold on to God's unchanging hand and follow, listen, wait upon his instruction(s) and through prayer and fasting (If you have never fasted, ask God how, what, and how long you should fast and wait for his instruction as he will lead and guide you). Watch what God will start doing and performing in your life. It will blow your mind as I am living witness and testimony!

7

The Catapulting

"Won't He Do It" by Koryn Hawthorne
"Speak the Name" by Koryn Hawthorne
"To Worship You I Live" by Israel Houghton
"I'm Getting Ready" by Tasha Cobbs
"You Covered Me" by Dr. R.A. Vernon & "The Word" Church Praise Team led by Tim Reddick
Let Your Power Fall—James Fortune & FIYA (featuring Zacardi Cortez)

> This is not a bakery. I don't sugarcoat anything. If you ask for my opinion…then that's what you'll get. Don't be mad when it's not what you want to hear. (work quotes)

> Should you ever find yourself the victim of other people's bitterness, smallness, or insecurities. Remember things could be worse…you could be them. (www.rawforbeauty.com)

> I don't chase anyone anymore. Wanna walk out of my life, there's the door. I'll even hold it open for you. (Wiz Khalifa)

Be the kind of woman that when your feet hit the floor each morning the devil says. Oh, crap, she's up!

—Unknown

The devil whispers, "You Can't Withstand the Storm." The warrior replied, "I am the storm."

—Anonymous

A successful woman is one who can build a firm foundation with the bricks others have thrown at her.

—Power of Positivity

Be grateful for your singleness. It has made you strong and independent and unflinching in your willingness to settle. It has protected you from wrong men and forced you to take risks and taught you the value of your own company. It has given you the space and grace to become exactly who you are. (Beautiful Uncertainty)

God spoke to me and said: You have been set apart for a reason. They don't understand your thought process. For I, the Lord Almighty have given you the mind that you have. They don't understand me; therefore, they don't understand you. Follow me, hold on and get ready, for the catapulting of my spirit anointing and power. You may not understand what I am doing and how I am performing it. Follow me (God) and trust me (God) for I am the Lord that created you and chose you when I planted you in your mother's womb. I chose you from the very beginning, again, that's why you never felt a part of any crowd or group that you were involved in because I set you apart from the beginning and knew exactly who you were and I know exactly what I have done and what I am doing. Your children are safe in my arms, so do the work that I have and will set before you. No more excuses and no more time. Your time is now and the hour has come for the prophetic word has been spoken, given, and imparted in you by me (the Almighty God).

One night as I was laying in bed, the Lord said to me, "Your organization will now go through a major transition in the spirit realm (God will give the warning)." I got up the next morning, got down on my knees, and prayed. I got up off my knees and talked to the Lord as I address him every morning with, "Good morning, Father, husband, and first true love, and tell him how much I love and adore him and thank him for loving me so much that he would choose me to talk to. I headed out to work and as I walked into my organization, there standing in the hallway, were two of my colleagues looking distraught and upset. I said good morning as they just stood there and just looked at me. I asked them if everything was okay, they looked at me, and said, "I just can't take this anymore." I told them to just hold on, it's going to be all right, and that we have to be the light in the darkness and continued down the hallway to my office.

One hour later, as I was heading to a meeting, another colleague from my former department informed me that another colleague was looking for me and had been looking for me all morning. I saw the colleague that had been looking for me. She grabbed my hand and asked me to please pray for her and proceeded to tell me why. I stopped her and informed her not to tell me and that I would pray for her and if it was meant for me to know, God would reveal it to me. Oftentimes we don't need to know what the prayer request is, you just ask, "God, whatever your will is, let your will be done and to do whatever the person who needs prayer is asking for and to give them the desires of their heart."

The employee who needed prayer came to me two days later, gave me a hug, thanked me, and said the she knew that I had been praying and that God did exactly what she was asking for. I in turn informed her not to thank me, thank God as God is the one who did it, and God used me as an open and willing vessel and that on no account did I do anything. The glory, honor, and praise all goes to God. I am nothing without him. I gave her a hug, told her that I loved her, and that God loved her more.

The following morning, I went into a friend's office (a woman of God who I have known for years and works for the same organization). As we proceeded in a discussion regarding work, another colleague walked into her office. This colleague never comes into her office anytime that I have been there (also a woman of God and a pastor of the church that she attends). She started to cry and pour out as we all talked and ended up laughing and the laughter turned into prayer. As we stood, holding hands and praying, the power of God filled the office as we all opened our eyes at the same time and just stared at each other. We all knew in the spirit what was happening. The Lord led me to lay hands, which is something that I have rarely done, and I have only done it as the Lord leads. As I laid hands and was speaking what the Lord led me to say to her, she started falling to the floor. My colleague and I held her up and sat her in the chair. We tried to stop praying and couldn't. Once God allowed us to finish, she turned to me and stared at me for a while as tears began to fall from her eyes. She shared that God had confirmed through me everything that she had been praying and asking him for.

Prior to the prayer and several months earlier, this same pastor stopped me in the hallway and told me that there was a mighty calling on my life and that God had me in preparation for the call and in preparation for my Boaz.

Several months earlier as I was at home, lying in bed, the Lord told me to consecrate and purify myself. I didn't know what that meant. I looked it up in the Word of God as well as Googled the meaning. Once I knew what it meant and what God was saying, I said, "Okay, Lord." Not realizing that one week prior to the Lord telling me that, I brought coconut milk, which I had never done and didn't know why I brought it. I went to church the following Sunday and talked to one of my church members, one who I am really close with, who is like an aunt to me, and informed her of what the Lord told me. She backed up and looked at me and said wow and laughed. I asked her why was she laughing and she said that it was about to be just me and God and that I was giving everything and all of me to GOD, and that this was the true calling and choosing and there is no turning back.

I bathed in coconut milk for two months straight every night as I said to the Lord, "I consecrate myself, I purify myself and saturate myself in you, Lord, Father God, and give you everything (myself, my children, my spirit, my soul, my heart, my dogs, my home, my career, my finances, my concerns, my fears, my tears, and my Boaz, whoever he may be). Lord, I totally belong to you and trust you with everything and everything within me and every fiber of my being. After one month of bathing in coconut milk, the Lord told me to now saturate myself from head to toe as I had only been consecrating, saturating, and purifying my body, and for another month (equaling two months), I saturated myself from head to toe saying, "I consecrate myself, I purify myself, and saturate myself in you Lord Father God and give you everything (myself, my children, my spirit, my soul, my heart, my dogs, my home, my career, my finances, my concerns, my fears, my tears and my Boaz whoever he may be) Lord, I totally belong to you and trust you with everything and everything within me and every fiber of my being.

After several weeks of consecrating, purifying, saturating, and giving myself to the Lord daily, I would come to work, and many colleagues kept telling me that I looked completely different and there was a glow unlike anything that they had ever seen before. I would just smile as only two people knew what the Lord had said to me and what the Lord told me to do. During the consecration, purification and saturation period, I would often fall asleep with the Word of God ministering in my ear or with music, mostly "The Call" by Isabel Davis; "Gracefully Broken" by Tasha Cobbs; "To Worship You I Live by Israel Houghton; or "Oceans" by Hillsong United. As I would wake in the morning during this period of time, my constant prayer was and has been, "God let me see people with your eyes. Allow me to love people the way that you love me, give me a heart like yours."

Once the Lord instructed me that my consecration period had been completed, the Lord told me that anyone who came to me of the opposite sex that wanted to date, asked for my phone number, or was seeking an intimate relationship, that I was not allowed to date or talk to anyone of the opposite sex on the phone, except for one person. One male friend of mine was the only male (besides my sons) that I could talk to on the phone or hold conversations with regarding life, God and what I wanted out of life. I never informed my friend that he was the only male that I was allowed to talk to on the phone or in person as I was and am adamant about following God's instructions.

As I continue to serve the Lord, I have been placed on many fasts and much prayer. God has and is continuing to show and teach me many things (as I asked God to be my teacher) as well as the nature, character, spirit, soul, and mind-set of many people that come in and out of my life. Even though some people who I may have wanted to stay in my life (within the last several months), God has allowed them to enter and exit for a reason (as I know that people enter your life for a reason, season, treason, or lifetime). I now realize in allowing God to be the pilot, driver, and director in and of my life, I am no longer my own nor am I in control of who, what, how, or why people and things come and go.

I also try not to ask or question God nor do I try to figure it out as I am human with a human heart with feelings.

One thing is for sure and two for certain, I know who and who's I am and I know God knows what he is doing and I trust God with my very life, heart, and soul.

I know that everybody and certain people and things can't go where God is taking you. It doesn't always feel good, but it's for your good, and all things and people serve and have a purpose. I am ready for the journey and for the up building of God's kingdom. It may not always be easy and may become quite difficult at times, and I know this is only the beginning as I say, "He (God) ain't done with me yet."

To Be Continued

About the Author

S andra Adona-Durham was born and raised in Prince Georges County, Maryland, and has worked in the medical field for the last fifteen years before writing her first book. As a first-time author of the book titled *From the Gutter to God's Pulpit*. A woman of God who shares her life experiences, hurts, heartbreaks, trials, tribulations, as well as many blessings that have been bestowed upon her children and herself with others, and letting all know. If God did it and is doing it for her, without a shadow of a doubt, God can certainly do it for you.

CPSIA information can be obtained
at www.ICGtesting.com
Printed in the USA
BVHW072155020321
601492BV00008B/853